CARL PEI

The Future in Your Hands: How the Nothing Phone (3)
is Set to Transform Your Smartphone Experience

Charles M. Blevins

Carl Pei

Copyright © 2025 by Charles M. Blevins All Rights Reserved

Carl Pei

DISCLAIMER

This book serves as an independent exploration of the life and accomplishments of Carl Pei. It is not associated with or approved by any other publications about him. The content is designed to offer readers a deeper insight into his journey and is intended solely for informational use. Readers are advised to confirm specific details on their own. This work is meant to complement existing resources rather than replace them.

Carl Pei

TABLE OF CONTENTS

Carl Pei

Introduction

What if the next smartphone you pick up doesn't just serve as a device but as a game-changer? Picture a world where your phone is more than just a tool—it's a seamless extension of who you are. A product that challenges the norm, strips away unnecessary complexity, and focuses entirely on the experience you deserve. This may sound like a far-reaching dream, but for Carl Pei, it's already in the making.

Carl Pei has quickly become a defining figure in the tech world, known for his bold approach, constant innovation, and unwavering desire to reshape the future of consumer technology. But his story goes beyond the typical narrative of an entrepreneur's rise. It's about someone who, against the odds, decided to create something that didn't just fit into the existing framework but completely redefined it. His journey hasn't followed the typical path, and the product that perfectly embodies this vision—the

Carl Pei

Nothing Phone (3)—is more than just another smartphone; it's a bold statement.

Pei's journey isn't just about the breakthroughs he's achieved or the companies he's built. It's about a relentless pursuit of creating a future where technology is not something that complicates our lives but something that enhances them. It's about making what's complicated feel simple, eliminating the clutter, and turning the mundane into something extraordinary. In a world where massive corporations churn out predictable devices year after year, Carl Pei's vision offers a refreshing alternative—a belief that technology can be intuitive, beautiful, and deeply meaningful.

This biography aims to take you behind the curtain of Carl Pei's life and career, offering a closer look at the mind that drove the creation of OnePlus and Nothing. It also uncovers the personal philosophies and life experiences that have shaped him into the visionary leader he is today. It's the story of a person who asked why things couldn't be different and then worked tirelessly to make that difference a reality.

In the current tech landscape, we often hear the term "disruptor" thrown around, but few individuals truly live up to that label as Carl Pei does. As a co-founder of OnePlus and the force behind Nothing, Pei has spent over a decade challenging the norm in the smartphone industry. This book isn't merely about the devices he's created or the companies he's founded. It's about understanding the deep-rooted philosophy behind his every move and how it could radically shift the way we engage with technology.

When Pei helped establish OnePlus in 2013, his mission was straightforward: to create a smartphone with premium features but without the inflated price tag. The result was the OnePlus One—a phone that quickly gained a loyal following due to its unbeatable combination of quality and affordability. This unconventional approach to smartphone manufacturing helped OnePlus quickly rise to global prominence and laid the groundwork for Pei's next venture—Nothing.

But Nothing is not just another tech company. It's built on the idea that technology shouldn't be an obstacle in our lives but should seamlessly integrate with how we live. With the launch of the Nothing Phone (1), Pei and his team turned heads with a unique design and focus on transparency and simplicity. Now, the Nothing Phone (3) is poised to push those boundaries even further, promising a smartphone that's not only functional but genuinely enjoyable to use.

This biography will explore the motivations, obstacles, and milestones in Pei's journey, offering a deep understanding of his mindset and vision. We will look at the decisions, both personal and professional, that led him to step away from OnePlus and create Nothing—an ambitious company set on challenging the tech world's expectations.

Carl Pei

Carl Pei's path has been one of growth, transformation, and resilience. From his early years in China to his key role in one of the most successful tech startups in the world, this book will offer an inside look at the factors that shaped his career. We will explore the guiding principles that have driven him, from his time at Oppo to his decision to break away from OnePlus and build something new. Through this journey, we'll see how Pei's dedication to design, user experience, and simplicity has been his guiding light, helping him navigate the ups and downs of building two iconic brands.

This book will also take a look at the man behind the brand, providing a rare glimpse into Carl Pei's personal life. What values guide him? What inspires his creativity? How does he see the role of technology in our daily lives? These questions will be explored as we paint a fuller picture of the person behind the innovations that are changing the way we use technology.

Carl Pei

Every chapter of this biography will bring you closer to understanding Carl Pei not just as a businessman but as a visionary. It's the story of a man whose philosophy could very well shape the future of consumer technology. From the early days at Oppo to the rise of OnePlus, and finally, to the launch of Nothing, we will explore the highs and lows of his journey, uncovering both his successes and struggles.

As you read, you'll not only learn about the groundbreaking work Pei has done but also gain insight into the mindset of one of the most influential figures in the tech world. This book promises to be a thoroughly researched, engaging exploration that will resonate with both tech enthusiasts and general readers alike. You'll discover not only the innovations he's spearheaded but also the approach he's taken toward life and work—a mindset that challenges conventional thinking in an industry that's often defined by tradition and routine.

Carl Pei

Beyond that, this biography offers a glimpse into the future of technology—a future where user experience takes center stage, where the line between human and machine blurs, and where simplicity rules. Through Pei's vision, we see a future where technology isn't just about utility but about joy. A future where our devices are not only smart—they are beautifully designed, intuitive, and delightful to use.

Carl Pei's journey is just beginning, and the Nothing Phone (3) is only the start. This biography offers you a chance to explore the past, present, and future of one of today's most exciting tech innovators, giving you an up-close look at the revolution unfolding right at your fingertips.

Carl Pei

Chapter 1

Who is Carl Pei?

Carl Pei is widely recognized for his groundbreaking role in the tech world, notably as a co-founder of OnePlus and the driving force behind the creation of Nothing. His career has been marked by a series of bold decisions that have reshaped the smartphone industry. However, his story begins long before he rose to prominence in the world of tech. His path was shaped by his unique upbringing, his experiences in two very different cultures, and the education that ultimately led him to a career at the intersection of business and technology.

Born on September 11, 1989, in Beijing, China, Carl Pei was exposed to two distinct cultures from an early age. His father, who was Chinese, and his mother, who was Swedish, gave him the opportunity to experience life from two perspectives. Growing up in Beijing during a time of tremendous change, Pei witnessed China's rapid transformation from a closed-off nation to a global economic powerhouse. This environment, with its palpable energy and constant development, had a profound effect on Pei, influencing his view of the world and his eventual entrepreneurial ambitions.

Despite his early immersion in a society focused on growth and progress, Pei's life was also deeply influenced by his Swedish heritage. The contrasting culture of Sweden, with its emphasis on equality, social welfare, and a more measured pace of life, offered Pei a unique lens through which he could examine the world. This combination of influences was pivotal in shaping his outlook on business and technology.

Pei's interest in technology was evident from a young age. Like many children, he was fascinated by gadgets and how they worked, but unlike many of his peers, Pei's curiosity wasn't just about functionality. He became intrigued by how technology could bring people together and simplify daily life. His parents, both intellectuals and professionals, nurtured his inquisitive nature, encouraging him to explore different fields of interest, including technology. Growing up in an environment where innovation was happening all around him, Pei began to see the potential of technology to bridge cultures and improve lives on a global scale.

However, Pei's childhood in Beijing would soon give way to a major shift in his life. At the age of nine, his family moved to Sweden. The transition from Beijing—a fast-paced, constantly evolving city—to Sweden's calm, organized lifestyle was significant. It was more than just a move from one country to another; it was an adjustment to a whole new way of life. This cultural shift was challenging but ultimately served as a crucial period of growth for Pei. It was in Sweden that Pei first learned to reconcile his two cultural identities. His Chinese background and his new life in Sweden would blend together to form a unique worldview that would later influence his work as an entrepreneur.

The differences between life in China and Sweden were striking, but they provided Pei with the opportunity to develop a versatile and adaptive mindset. Where Beijing was a bustling metropolis brimming with energy and change, Sweden's quieter, more reflective approach to life allowed Pei to observe a different way of thinking about work, life, and business. These contrasting experiences were not only formative—they also gave him the tools to navigate challenges with a broader perspective.

In Sweden, the social environment was quite different from that in Beijing. Swedish culture places a high value on work-life balance, equality, and sustainability—values that Pei would carry with him throughout his professional life. These ideals helped shape his understanding of business as something that should not just generate profit, but also add value to society. The idea of integrating ethical and sustainable practices into business models was something Pei came to appreciate in Sweden, and it would play a key role in the way he later approached entrepreneurship.

Pei's relocation from China to Sweden was not just a physical move; it was a significant moment in his life that affected how he thought about the world and how he would approach both business and personal challenges. The contrast between the two countries highlighted the importance of adaptability and resilience. As a young boy, transitioning from one culture to another was not always easy, but it proved to be a formative experience that helped Pei develop a broad outlook on the world.

Living in Sweden exposed him to a different educational philosophy, which emphasized independent thought, creativity, and collaboration. This was a stark contrast to the more traditional, rigid structures of schooling in China. In Sweden, students were encouraged to ask questions, challenge ideas, and think critically— skills that Pei would later apply in his career as a tech entrepreneur. Sweden's educational system also placed a significant focus on developing students' ability to work together, an essential quality for anyone looking to succeed in the modern business world.

These early experiences—shifting between the fast-paced, dynamic environment of Beijing and the calm, structured environment of Sweden—helped Pei develop an open-minded approach to problem-solving. It allowed him to see business and technology from multiple viewpoints, understanding that solutions are not one-size-fits-all but need to account for a variety of factors, including cultural context. This insight would later help Pei make critical decisions as he navigated the competitive world of the tech industry.

Carl Pei's educational journey continued in Sweden when he enrolled at the Stockholm School of Economics (SSE). The decision to attend SSE was a pivotal one, as it would provide him with a deeper understanding of business, strategy, and economics—knowledge he would later use to shape his career. While his primary interest was in technology, Pei recognized that an education in business was crucial for turning his ideas into reality.

At SSE, Pei was exposed to a broad range of ideas that challenged traditional business thinking. The school's emphasis on entrepreneurship and innovation helped Pei understand that business was not just about running a company—it was about identifying opportunities, solving problems, and creating value for people. This perspective would shape the way he approached the development of OnePlus and, later, Nothing.

Despite his academic focus on business, Pei's passion for technology remained central to his interests. During his time at SSE, he realized that the future of business was intertwined with the advancement of technology. More than just gadgets, technology had the potential to reshape entire industries and impact the way people lived. Pei became increasingly fascinated by the role that smartphones played in people's daily lives and began thinking about how he could contribute to the future of this technology.

Pei's time at SSE was not just about academics—it was also about networking and finding like-minded individuals who shared his passion for innovation. During his time at the university, Pei met Pete Lau, who would later become his co-founder at OnePlus. The two quickly connected over their shared vision of creating a smartphone that combined high-end features with affordability. Their partnership, born out of mutual respect and a shared passion for technology, would eventually lead to the creation of OnePlus, a company that would forever change the smartphone industry.

Chapter 2

Carl Pei's Introduction to the Tech World – The Oppo Experience

Carl Pei's entry into the tech industry began with a formative period at Oppo, one of China's most prominent and influential smartphone manufacturers. His time with the company provided him with invaluable insights into the world of technology, particularly consumer electronics, global marketing, and the intricacies of international expansion. The experience he gained at Oppo helped shape his understanding of what it takes to succeed in an industry driven by innovation and competition, while also laying the foundation for his future entrepreneurial ventures.

Before Pei became a household name through OnePlus and later Nothing, his career took off at Oppo, a company at the time still striving to establish its presence outside of China. His years there were pivotal in both his personal and professional growth, offering a front-row seat to the complexities of the tech world. From navigating fierce competition to spearheading international campaigns, Pei's role in Oppo's development was instrumental in honing his skills and preparing him for the next big challenges in his career.

Carl Pei's journey into technology began when he joined Oppo, a company that was relatively unknown to many outsides of China at that point. Oppo, which had initially focused on producing other electronics like MP3 players and DVD players, was in the process of transitioning to the smartphone market. This shift presented a unique opportunity for Pei to step into an emerging industry, and he quickly became involved with Oppo's efforts to carve out a space in the increasingly competitive smartphone sector.

Carl Pei

When Pei joined Oppo in 2010, the company was beginning to make significant strides in its bid to challenge the established giants like Apple and Samsung. Although Oppo had already earned a solid reputation in the Chinese market, it had yet to break through internationally. It was during this pivotal moment that Pei was able to leverage his skills in marketing, strategy, and product development. This period marked the beginning of Pei's deep immersion in the rapidly evolving tech world, where he would learn firsthand the challenges and opportunities that come with scaling a technology company.

Oppo was far from the powerhouse it is today, but Pei saw its potential. The company was in the midst of shifting its focus from local markets to global expansion, and Pei recognized the significance of this transition. His time at Oppo was marked by his hands-on involvement in numerous aspects of the business, from product development to market strategy, and it gave him a front-row seat to the kind of innovation that drives the tech industry forward. While the company was still in its early stages of becoming a global competitor, Pei's role would soon prove to be pivotal in guiding Oppo's international efforts.

Working at Oppo exposed Carl Pei to some of the most important lessons in consumer technology, branding, and market strategy. As a company looking to make its mark on the global stage, Oppo faced immense competition from the world's largest tech companies. Pei's time at Oppo offered critical insights into the importance of understanding consumer needs, building strong brand identities, and creating products that not only met but exceeded expectations.

One of the most significant lessons Pei learned during his tenure at Oppo was the importance of consumer-centered product development. In a saturated market, simply creating a functional product was not enough; the key to success was understanding what consumers truly wanted. Oppo's initial challenges in the smartphone market were primarily about finding that sweet spot—developing a product that could appeal to a broad audience while maintaining high standards of quality and innovation. Pei quickly understood that in order to stand out, a product had to offer more than just impressive specifications—it had to provide an experience that spoke directly to the consumer.

This lesson would become fundamental to Pei's future work, particularly when he co-founded OnePlus. Pei's experience at Oppo reinforced the idea that technology should serve the user, not the other way around. He realized that great design and user experience were just as important as the technical specs of a product. Oppo's approach to developing smartphones with a focus on user satisfaction, particularly its emphasis on high-quality camera features, was a strategy that Pei would later adopt in his own ventures.

Another important lesson for Pei was the role of branding and identity in the tech industry. When Pei arrived at Oppo, the company had not yet established a strong global presence, and much of the branding and marketing were still in their infancy. As Oppo began to explore international markets, it became clear to Pei that the company needed to differentiate itself in a crowded marketplace. He learned that building a brand was about more than just designing products—it was about creating a story that resonated with people. Oppo's eventual success in global markets can be attributed to its ability to communicate a compelling message to consumers, a lesson that Pei would carry forward as he worked to build OnePlus into a global brand.

The experiences Pei gained at Oppo also helped him understand the importance of adaptability and flexibility in business. In a constantly changing industry, the ability to pivot and respond to new challenges was crucial. Oppo's approach to international expansion required Pei to adjust marketing strategies and product offerings based on the unique demands of each market. This level of adaptability became an essential component of Pei's approach to business, and it was one of the factors that contributed to the success of OnePlus and, later, Nothing.

Pei's work at Oppo was not just confined to product development; his role in the company's international expansion was one of his most defining contributions. At the time, Oppo was relatively unknown outside of China, and its goal was to build a brand that could compete with the likes of Apple and Samsung. Pei's expertise in marketing and global strategy played a central role in Oppo's efforts to grow its presence in international markets.

Pei understood that in order to succeed globally, Oppo needed to craft a marketing strategy that was both innovative and adaptable. It wasn't enough to simply take the same approach used in China and apply it to other regions. Instead, Pei and his team worked to tailor their campaigns to the specific needs and preferences of each market. This involved understanding the cultural nuances and consumer behaviors in different regions and adjusting their messaging accordingly. Pei's ability to navigate these complexities and craft campaigns that resonated with diverse audiences was instrumental in helping Oppo build a successful international brand.

One of the key elements of Oppo's marketing strategy that Pei helped develop was the focus on the camera. At a time when mobile photography was becoming an increasingly important feature for smartphone users, Oppo made a strategic decision to focus its efforts on delivering high-quality camera experiences. Pei recognized that, while many smartphones on the market were offering similar specifications, Oppo had the opportunity to differentiate itself by excelling in a key area that consumers cared about—the camera. This focus on high-quality photography became one of Oppo's defining features, setting the brand apart from its competitors and appealing to a wide range of consumers.

In addition to product innovation, Pei also played a crucial role in establishing relationships with key distributors, retailers, and partners around the world. Expanding into new markets required navigating complex distribution networks, and Pei's ability to build these partnerships was key to Oppo's international success. His work in securing retail agreements and forging strategic alliances helped Oppo ensure that its products reached a global audience.

Pei's strategic thinking in marketing and international expansion helped Oppo build a foundation that would allow the company to expand rapidly in global markets. By focusing on user needs, tailoring marketing strategies, and building strong relationships with partners, Pei played an essential role in shaping Oppo's growth and laying the groundwork for its eventual success as one of the largest smartphone manufacturers in the world.

Carl Pei

Chapter 3

Building OnePlus – From Concept to Global Phenomenon

The story of OnePlus is not simply one of a startup entering a competitive market—it is a journey defined by ambition, vision, and the courage to challenge industry giants. It is a narrative built on a belief that quality doesn't have to come at a steep price. This journey began with Carl Pei and Pete Lau, two individuals with a shared vision of creating smartphones that combine top-tier performance with accessibility. The path from an idea to a globally recognized brand was not straightforward. It was marked by hurdles that tested the resilience of its founders, but these challenges ultimately laid the foundation for the success of OnePlus, especially with the launch of the OnePlus One. This device set the stage for a revolution in the smartphone market, signaling the arrival of a new player that was ready to redefine expectations in terms of both performance and value.

The inception of OnePlus came about due to a simple but powerful observation. Carl Pei and Pete Lau, both of whom had extensive experience at Oppo, recognized a gap in the market. In an industry dominated by Apple and Samsung, consumers had limited options if they wanted premium features at an affordable price. For many, the flagship phones offered by these brands came with a hefty price tag, often leaving those seeking high-end performance with limited alternatives. Pei and Lau were determined to change that by creating a device that offered similar or better specifications without the inflated costs associated with flagship devices.

OnePlus was founded in December 2013, and its mission was clear: to offer top-notch smartphones without compromising on quality or making consumers pay a premium. The idea was to craft a smartphone that could compete with the best on the market but come at a fraction of the price. Although the concept seemed simple, executing it was far from easy. At the time, the smartphone market was heavily saturated, and it would take more than just a great product to stand out. Pei and Lau faced significant obstacles—ranging from securing funding to managing manufacturing logistics. They were starting from scratch, with limited resources, and had to rely heavily on the expertise and support of Oppo, which helped them with production and logistics.

The team behind OnePlus, despite facing these early challenges, never wavered in their belief that they could create something unique. Their breakthrough came with the release of the OnePlus One in 2014, a device that exceeded expectations and demonstrated that a high-quality smartphone did not have to come with an exorbitant price tag. The OnePlus One delivered premium features—large screen size, powerful processing, and high-quality cameras—at a price that made it accessible to a larger segment of consumers.

Although the OnePlus One was a success, the journey had not been without its struggles. In the early stages, OnePlus faced significant pressure to prove itself, especially in the face of more established competitors. From securing initial funding to navigating complex international markets, the path forward was not always smooth. Yet, every challenge served to refine the company's approach, and the perseverance shown by Pei, Lau, and the team would eventually pay off. The OnePlus One's success became the turning point that allowed OnePlus to evolve from an ambitious startup to a respected brand in the smartphone industry.

The OnePlus One's impact on the smartphone industry cannot be overstated. Prior to its release, the smartphone market was dominated by a few major players, and the idea of delivering flagship-level features at an affordable price was seen as an almost impossible challenge. However, OnePlus proved that this was not only possible but could be done without compromising on quality or performance.

At the time of its release, the OnePlus One was revolutionary. It delivered a superior user experience while still being priced significantly lower than its competitors. The phone featured a large display, fast processing power, and an advanced camera, positioning it as a true flagship device. But what truly set the OnePlus One apart was its pricing strategy. OnePlus sold the phone at a fraction of the cost of its competitors, challenging the traditional pricing models of the smartphone industry.

The success of the OnePlus One signaled a shift in consumer expectations. Prior to this, consumers were accustomed to paying a premium for flagship devices, with the belief that higher prices were synonymous with better quality. OnePlus's approach challenged this notion, showing that premium smartphones could be offered at a more accessible price point. This not only helped OnePlus attract a loyal following but also forced other manufacturers to reconsider their pricing strategies. The OnePlus One made it clear that high-quality smartphones did not have to be prohibitively expensive, and it marked a turning point in the industry's approach to pricing.

Beyond its performance and pricing, the OnePlus One also made waves with its design and user experience. The device was sleek, elegant, and intuitive, setting a new standard for what consumers expected in terms of smartphone design. By focusing on delivering a high-quality product without the unnecessary features that many other companies included, OnePlus built a device that was both practical and aesthetically pleasing. The phone became a favorite among tech enthusiasts, and its launch helped establish OnePlus as a serious contender in the smartphone market.

One of the key factors behind OnePlus's success was its innovative and non-traditional marketing strategy. Unlike many of the more established players in the smartphone market, OnePlus did not rely on massive advertising budgets or TV commercials to promote its devices. Instead, the company focused on building an online community and using word-of-mouth marketing to spread the word about its products.

OnePlus's marketing strategy was centered around creating a sense of exclusivity and community. Early on, the company introduced an invitation system for purchasing the OnePlus One. The invitation system made the phone feel like a limited-edition product, creating a sense of urgency and excitement among potential buyers. Consumers had to be invited to purchase the device, which generated buzz and created anticipation. The strategy also helped to build a community of early adopters who felt they were part of something special. This sense of exclusivity helped OnePlus generate interest and created a loyal customer base that would continue to support the brand in the years to come.

In addition to the invitation system, OnePlus relied heavily on online forums, social media, and community-driven marketing. The company engaged directly with its audience through platforms like Reddit, where users could ask questions, provide feedback, and share their experiences. This direct interaction with customers helped to build trust and foster a sense of community among OnePlus users. The company listened to its customers and incorporated their feedback into future products, ensuring that the devices met the needs and expectations of the people who used them.

The slogan "Never Settle" became the heart of OnePlus's marketing efforts. This phrase encapsulated the company's philosophy of delivering the best possible product without compromise. "Never Settle" resonated deeply with tech enthusiasts who were dissatisfied with the high prices and limited options in the smartphone market. OnePlus used this message not just in its advertising but as a central theme that guided its product development, design philosophy, and consumer interactions.

The "Never Settle" philosophy was more than just a slogan—it became the company's rallying cry. It

Carl Pei

symbolized OnePlus's commitment to pushing boundaries and offering consumers the best possible value without cutting corners. This philosophy helped OnePlus stand out in a crowded market and attracted a loyal following of customers who shared the company's vision.

Another crucial part of OnePlus's marketing strategy was its focus on transparency. The company was upfront about its goals, challenges, and achievements, which helped to build trust with consumers. OnePlus's transparency, combined with its community-driven approach, created an authentic brand identity that stood out in a market often criticized for its corporate opacity.

Chapter 4

Leaving OnePlus – A New Chapter Begins

Carl Pei's story in the tech world is closely intertwined with the success of OnePlus, a company he co-founded and helped catapult into global recognition. However, after years of significant contributions, Pei made the difficult decision to part ways with OnePlus in 2020, marking a pivotal shift in his career. His departure was not the end of his journey but the beginning of a new chapter, one that would lead him to the creation of a new company: Nothing. This decision was driven by his desire for a fresh start, his growing frustration with the direction OnePlus was taking, and his broader vision for the future of technology.

Carl Pei

Leaving OnePlus was a deeply personal and professional decision for Carl Pei. After co-founding the company with Pete Lau in 2013, Pei was an essential figure in its growth, helping to define the company's identity and market strategy. The OnePlus One, the company's debut product, was a breakthrough, challenging the idea that high-end smartphones had to come with a hefty price tag. The company quickly became a favorite among tech enthusiasts, and Pei played a key role in its success. However, despite the company's rapid growth and recognition, Pei began to feel a disconnect between his own ambitions and the direction OnePlus was heading.

Pei's departure was influenced by several factors. Over time, he began to sense a divergence in vision between himself and the leadership at OnePlus, particularly Pete Lau. While Pei remained focused on innovating and breaking boundaries in the tech industry, he noticed that OnePlus was increasingly shifting its focus to compete directly with mainstream brands like Apple and Samsung.

The company's model was becoming more conventional, with an emphasis on expanding market share and catering to the mass market rather than exploring disruptive innovation.

This shift in focus left Pei feeling restricted. He had always believed in the power of technology to change the world, but the more he observed OnePlus's trajectory, the more he realized that his vision for the future of tech no longer aligned with the company's goals. Pei's frustration stemmed from the fact that he felt the industry had become saturated with incremental upgrades rather than bold, game-changing ideas. He was determined to continue challenging the status quo in tech, and for that, he felt he needed to step away from OnePlus.

Another contributing factor to his decision was his desire for greater creative freedom. Over the years, Pei had established himself as a visionary in the tech world, but at OnePlus, he was operating within a structured environment that came with limitations. As OnePlus grew, it became more corporate, and Pei began to feel constrained by the company's organizational framework. He wanted to be free to pursue new, uncharted opportunities without being held back by the constraints of a large, established company. In many ways, his departure was a realization that to truly innovate and explore his full potential, he needed to take a leap into something completely new.

Leaving OnePlus was, therefore, not an easy decision, but it was one that Pei felt was necessary to move forward with his personal and professional growth. The decision marked a turning point in his career, but it also represented a return to his roots: a desire to create products that could truly change people's lives through innovation.

After parting ways with OnePlus, Pei wasted no time in pursuing his next venture, which would soon become Nothing. His decision to launch this new company was not simply a desire to create another tech brand but rather an opportunity to build something that would break the mold. Pei's vision for Nothing was deeply rooted in his dissatisfaction with the current state of consumer technology. He felt that the industry had grown stale, with many companies offering similar products that lacked the innovation and excitement of the early days of smartphones.

Pei's new company, Nothing, was conceived as a response to this frustration. He wanted to create a brand that would prioritize user experience and design while offering something entirely fresh to the tech market. The idea behind Nothing was to strip away the complexities and clutter that had come to define many tech products, focusing instead on simplicity, elegance, and seamless integration. Pei believed that consumers were increasingly looking for technology that didn't overwhelm them with features but instead complemented their lives in meaningful and intuitive ways.

Nothing's debut was far from conventional, and this reflected Pei's broader philosophy of challenging industry norms. From the outset, he wanted the company to be something different—not just another tech brand but a company with a unique identity that connected with consumers on a deeper level. Nothing's approach to design and branding would prioritize aesthetics and experience over mere functionality. Pei believed that tech products should be more than tools; they should be beautiful, desirable, and easy to use. His aim was not only to create another product but to introduce a new way of thinking about consumer electronics.

The launch of Nothing marked a return to Pei's roots as a designer and innovator. Unlike his work at OnePlus, where his contributions were part of a broader team effort, Pei now had the freedom to shape the company's vision from the ground up. This freedom allowed him to push the boundaries of what was possible in tech, experimenting with new ideas and designs that he believed would resonate with consumers.

Carl Pei

Pei's first major product after leaving OnePlus was the Nothing Ear (1), which launched in 2021. The earbuds exemplified the core philosophy of the brand: sleek, minimalist design combined with cutting-edge technology. The product stood out not only for its performance but also for its unique look, featuring a transparent design that made the internal components visible. This product symbolized the future of Nothing: a blend of simplicity and sophistication that spoke to both aesthetics and functionality.

In building Nothing, Pei sought to create an ecosystem of products that would work together seamlessly. He envisioned a future where technology was not fragmented but connected, offering consumers a holistic experience that spanned various categories, from audio devices to smartphones and beyond. The aim was to create products that felt intuitive and natural, products that were more than just gadgets but were woven into the fabric of daily life.

Carl Pei

The creation of Nothing was driven by Pei's deep desire to return to the roots of innovation and to create products that pushed the boundaries of what was possible in consumer technology. Pei had grown disillusioned with the traditional model of tech companies, where the focus was primarily on incremental improvements and profitability rather than on genuinely groundbreaking ideas. The industry, in his view, had become stagnant, with many companies merely adding features to existing products without considering the broader needs of consumers.

At the heart of Nothing's vision was a commitment to simplicity and user-centered design. Pei believed that technology had become too complex, with too many features that overwhelmed users rather than enhancing their experience. With Nothing, he sought to create products that were elegant, functional, and easy to use. His aim was to deliver an experience that was intuitive, where technology didn't get in the way but instead integrated seamlessly into the user's life.

Pei's motivation for founding Nothing was also rooted in a desire to challenge the status quo in the tech industry. He felt that large, established companies had become complacent, focusing too much on profit margins and market share rather than on innovation. Nothing was his response to this, a company that would not follow the typical corporate playbook but instead focus on creating products that mattered to people. Pei was not just interested in making gadgets—he wanted to make meaningful technology that would make a difference in how people lived and interacted with the world around them.

The name Nothing itself reflected this philosophy. Pei wanted the brand to stand for simplicity and clarity, stripping away unnecessary complexity. The idea was to create products that felt natural and effortless, a reflection of the user's lifestyle rather than something that required constant management or adjustment. Nothing was not about adding more to the market but about offering a new approach to how technology could work for people.

Carl Pei

For Pei, founding Nothing was a chance to break free from the limitations of his previous role at OnePlus and to pursue a new vision, one that was not confined by the boundaries of the smartphone market. He wanted to build an ecosystem of products that would shape the future of tech, combining design, performance, and user experience in a way that had not been done before. This was a vision of technology that went beyond just making better products—it was about making technology more human, more intuitive, and more meaningful.

Carl Pei

Chapter 5

The Birth of Nothing – A New Era in Consumer Tech

The launch of Nothing marked a new and pivotal moment in the consumer technology landscape. Founded by Carl Pei, who previously co-founded OnePlus, the company emerged with a distinct vision that sought to challenge the status quo of the tech industry. Nothing was not just another brand entering an already crowded market; it was a bold attempt to reshape the way we view and interact with technology. Pei's ambition with Nothing was to reimagine consumer electronics in a way that prioritized simplicity, design, and innovation. The foundation of this new company would soon materialize in a product that would stand out: the Nothing Ear (1), an innovative pair of wireless earbuds that would catch the attention of consumers and critics alike.

Carl Pei

The creation of Nothing was driven by a desire to disrupt the consumer technology industry. Carl Pei saw an opportunity to create a brand that would stand apart from the noise of larger, established tech companies. His motivation stemmed from a growing frustration with the direction of the industry, which had become overly complex, profit-driven, and focused on incremental advancements rather than truly innovative products. As a result, Pei sought to build a company that would emphasize user experience, simplicity, and innovation.

Nothing's mission from its inception was clear: to simplify technology and make it more accessible, intuitive, and human. Pei's vision for the company was to remove the clutter of modern tech—products that were packed with features that consumers didn't need or couldn't use. Instead, Nothing would create products that were clean, simple, and focused on improving the user's life, not overwhelming them with unnecessary complexity.

The core values of Nothing reflects this vision. First and foremost was simplicity. Pei and his team aimed to design products that were as user-friendly as possible, with a focus on functionality without excess. By stripping away the unnecessary, they wanted to provide devices that were intuitive, easy to navigate, and enjoyable to use. This commitment to simplicity was not just about the appearance of products but also about how they functioned, with the goal of ensuring that users could interact with technology effortlessly.

Transparency was another cornerstone of the company's values. Pei was determined to build a brand that was open with its customers. Nothing would not only provide high-quality products but also communicate openly about how they were designed, produced, and distributed. The goal was to foster trust with consumers, allowing them to feel confident that Nothing was a brand built on integrity and authenticity.

Lastly, community played a significant role in the company's mission. Pei recognized that technology is not just about the products themselves but the relationships between brands and their customers. Nothing would be a brand that engaged directly with its user base, listening to feedback and building products that reflected the desires and needs of the people who used them. Creating a sense of belonging was just as important as creating great products, and Pei wanted to establish a company that would resonate with users on an emotional level.

Together, these values of simplicity, transparency, and community would define Nothing and serve as the foundation for everything the company would build. Pei's vision was not just about making devices—it was about creating a brand that could change the way we thought about technology, making it more connected to our lives, easier to use, and more reflective of who we are as consumers.

Carl Pei

One of the key elements that set Nothing apart from other tech companies was its distinct design philosophy. Pei's approach to design was rooted in the belief that technology should be both functional and beautiful, and that the two should not be mutually exclusive. Nothing's products, from the outset, were intended to be aesthetically pleasing while also offering cutting-edge performance. The design philosophy was about more than just making products look good—it was about creating a deeper connection between the user and the technology.

A central feature of Nothing's design philosophy was the emphasis on simplicity. Pei wanted to create products that felt intuitive, easy to use, and uncluttered. The devices were designed to eliminate unnecessary features, focusing only on what truly enhanced the user experience. This minimalist approach was reflected in the company's first product, the Nothing Ear (1). The earbuds were designed with clean lines, a transparent body, and a focus on user comfort. The transparency of the earbuds was a deliberate choice, not just to make them visually striking, but to symbolize the company's commitment to openness and honesty. By allowing users to see the internal components, Nothing was saying that it had nothing to hide—its design was as transparent as its business practices.

The minimalist aesthetic of the products also served to emphasize functionality over excess. Many consumer tech products, particularly in the audio market, were designed with features that complicated the user experience. Nothing, on the other hand, sought to streamline the experience, offering consumers a product that was simple to operate, comfortable to use, and of exceptional quality without being weighed down by unnecessary features. The design was focused on delivering a premium user experience without adding complexity or confusion.

Another key element of Nothing's design philosophy was sustainability. In a world where consumer electronics are often criticized for their environmental impact,

Nothing made it a point to minimize its ecological footprint. The company used sustainable materials wherever possible, reduced packaging waste, and made conscious efforts to ensure that its manufacturing processes were environmentally friendly. Pei's commitment to creating products that were not only beautiful and functional but also responsible, was a significant part of Nothing's ethos. This approach resonated with consumers who were increasingly looking for companies that prioritized sustainability in their product designs.

Nothing's design language was about offering consumers an experience that was intuitive, visually appealing, and environmentally responsible. The combination of simplicity, transparency, and sustainability helped Nothing stand out in an industry that often focused on adding more features or making products that were difficult for users to engage with. Pei's philosophy was clear: technology should be accessible, transparent, and beautiful, with a focus on enriching the user experience rather than complicating it.

The Nothing Ear (1) was the first major product to be released by Nothing, and its announcement was highly anticipated. Given Carl Pei's established reputation in the tech world, particularly for his work with OnePlus, the launch of the Nothing Ear (1) generated a great deal of buzz. The wireless earbuds were the first tangible manifestation of Pei's vision for the brand and had a lot riding on them.

What set the Nothing Ear (1) apart from other wireless earbuds was not just its performance but its design. The transparent casing was an instant eye-catching feature, and it was this bold design choice that immediately set the product apart in the crowded audio market. The Ear (1) was not just another pair of wireless earbuds—it was a product that visually communicated the company's philosophy of openness, transparency, and simplicity. The decision to make the internal components visible was a deliberate move to break away from the typical opaque designs that dominated consumer electronics. It was a statement about how technology could be more honest and accessible to consumers.

In terms of performance, the Nothing Ear (1) lived up to the expectations. The earbuds featured active noise cancellation, solid sound quality, and long battery life—key features that would appeal to tech enthusiasts and casual users alike. What made the Ear (1) particularly remarkable, however, was how it combined these high-end features with an affordable price point. This was a core part of Nothing's value proposition: delivering premium technology at a more accessible price, challenging the pricing conventions of the consumer electronics market.

The initial reception to the Nothing Ear (1) was overwhelmingly positive. Critics praised the design, which was both sleek and functional, and the sound quality, which rivaled other higher-end wireless earbuds.

Carl Pei

The transparency of the earbuds was a hit with consumers, who appreciated the unique and futuristic look that set them apart from typical tech products. The launch was seen as a bold statement in the audio market, and Nothing quickly garnered a following of loyal customers who were drawn not only to the product's design but also to the company's philosophy.

One of the key takeaways from the launch was how effectively Nothing had managed to create a sense of excitement and anticipation around the product. Unlike many tech companies that rely on traditional marketing methods, Nothing used social media, influencer partnerships, and community-driven campaigns to build hype around the Ear (1). The company's emphasis on creating a transparent relationship with its customers helped foster trust and enthusiasm, and the success of the Ear (1) showed that there was a strong demand for products that prioritized simplicity, design, and performance.

Carl Pei

The release of the Nothing Ear (1) was just the beginning for the company. It served as a powerful demonstration of Pei's vision for a brand that could redefine what it meant to create consumer electronics. The positive reception of the earbuds solidified Nothing's place in the tech world and set the stage for future products that would continue to challenge industry norms.

Chapter 6

The Nothing Phone (1) – An Industry Disruptor

In 2022, the Nothing Phone (1) was unveiled, marking a significant moment in the world of consumer technology. Created by Carl Pei's company, Nothing, this device was designed to do much more than just compete in the crowded smartphone market. The Nothing Phone (1) set out to redefine how smartphones should look, feel, and interact with users. With its introduction, Pei and his team aimed to shake up an industry that, by many accounts, had grown stagnant and predictable. By combining cutting-edge design with an innovative user experience, the Nothing Phone (1) sought to disrupt the status quo and establish a new standard for the industry.

Carl Pei

The road to developing the Nothing Phone (1) was not one taken lightly by the team behind it. While Nothing had already made waves with the release of their first product, the Nothing Ear (1), creating a smartphone was a completely new challenge. But for Carl Pei, the decision to move into smartphones was a natural progression. The goal was to create a device that was unlike anything else in the market—a product that would be visually striking, user-friendly, and stand out from the overwhelming sameness that had come to characterize modern smartphones.

The development process focused heavily on design. The Nothing Phone (1) wasn't just another phone—it was meant to be a statement. At the heart of the phone was a design philosophy that emphasized transparency. The company decided on a transparent back that revealed the internal components of the device, a bold choice in an industry where internal components are usually hidden behind sleek, uniform exteriors. This transparency wasn't just a design gimmick; it symbolized Nothing's commitment to openness and authenticity. It was about showing consumers what they were getting, both in terms of technology and philosophy.

Along with its distinctive back design, the phone was equipped with impressive hardware specifications. Featuring a 120Hz OLED display, a Snapdragon 778G+ chipset, and a 50MP camera, the Nothing Phone (1) packed a punch in terms of performance. The 4,500mAh battery offered long-lasting power, while the 33W fast charging ensured that users wouldn't have to wait long for a boost. Despite its relatively affordable price tag, the phone delivered features that were on par with other mid-range smartphones, making it an attractive option for those who wanted quality without breaking the bank.

As Nothing moved forward with its plan, anticipation built around the phone's launch. The company, already known for creating a buzz with its marketing strategies, kept the phone under wraps, releasing teasers and sneak peeks leading up to the big reveal. The company's approach to marketing was consistent with its ethos: minimalist, focused on the product, and aimed at sparking curiosity rather than relying on over-the-top campaigns.

The official launch in July 2022 was met with great excitement. The phone's design, which included the transparent back and innovative features, was unlike anything seen in the smartphone industry in recent years. The phone was positioned as a fresh alternative to the mainstream products of Apple and Samsung, catering to tech enthusiasts who were looking for something unique.

The Nothing Phone (1) brought a radical shift in how smartphones were designed and how they could be used. The transparent back, featuring exposed components, was one of the most visible and talked-about features. For many, it wasn't just an aesthetic choice; it was a bold statement about the brand's approach to transparency in both product design and business practices. Unlike most smartphones, which hide their internal components, the Nothing Phone (1) invited users to experience the inner workings of their device in a visually appealing way. This design choice added an element of intrigue and engagement that wasn't typically found in smartphones.

But the design was more than just the transparent back. The phone's overall look was minimalist, with smooth lines and a compact build that made it comfortable to hold. Unlike the increasingly large and unwieldy smartphones of the day, the Nothing Phone (1) was designed to be sleek and easy to use. Its size, weight, and feel were considered in every aspect of the device's design, ensuring that it was not only functional but also ergonomic.

Beyond just the physical design, the Nothing Phone (1) also revolutionized the way users interacted with their devices. The Glyph Interface, a set of LED lights on the back of the phone, was perhaps the most distinctive feature in terms of user experience. These lights were not just for decoration—they served a functional purpose by notifying users of incoming calls, messages, and other alerts. The pattern and intensity of the lights could be customized, allowing users to assign different light sequences to different contacts or notification types. This personalization offered a new level of interactivity, making the phone feel more connected to the user in a way that other smartphones did not.

The phone's user interface was also designed with simplicity in mind. The software was based on a clean, near-stock version of Android, with minimal bloatware. The focus was on creating a smooth, fast, and intuitive user experience, avoiding the unnecessary features that often bog down smartphones from other manufacturers. The result was a device that was easy to navigate and enjoyable to use. Nothing's design philosophy was about stripping away distractions and providing an experience that was centered on what mattered most to the user.

In terms of its performance, the Nothing Phone (1) exceeded expectations for a mid-range device. The 120Hz OLED display provided vibrant colors and sharp contrasts, delivering a visually stunning experience for everything from browsing the web to watching videos. The phone's smooth scrolling and responsiveness made it a pleasure to interact with, and the high refresh rate ensured that the display was fluid, even during fast-paced activities like gaming.

The camera, another area where smartphones are often judged, was equipped with a 50MP sensor that produced crisp, clear photos with vivid colors. While it didn't necessarily outshine the flagship cameras of Apple and Samsung, it provided more than enough quality for everyday use, particularly given the price point of the device. The camera's ability to capture detailed images and videos was a significant selling point for the Nothing Phone (1), showing that users didn't have to pay a premium to get great photography capabilities.

All in all, the Nothing Phone (1) was a device that placed a premium on design and user experience. Every aspect of the phone, from its transparent design to its intuitive software, was crafted with the goal of making technology feel more human and approachable. By rethinking the way a smartphone should look, feel, and function, Nothing challenged the conventions of the smartphone industry and offered users a fresh alternative to the mainstream options on the market.

The reception of the Nothing Phone (1) was met with significant excitement and enthusiasm from both the tech community and consumers. As a product that broke from the typical smartphone mold, it garnered attention for its bold design, transparent back, and user-friendly interface. The phone's design, which was both innovative and aesthetically pleasing, was one of the primary factors that fueled its positive reception.

Critics were particularly impressed by the phone's visual appeal. The transparent back and Glyph Interface were standout features that set the device apart from others in the market. The exposed components of the phone, combined with the customizable LED light patterns, made the phone feel more like a piece of wearable technology than just a simple smartphone. This unique design resonated with many consumers, who saw it as a refreshing change from the sleek, opaque designs that had become the norm in the smartphone industry.

The phone's performance, especially given its mid-range pricing, was also praised. Reviewers noted that the Nothing Phone (1) offered a smooth, fast, and reliable user experience, rivaling more expensive flagship phones. The 120Hz OLED display, powerful chipset, and solid camera made it a highly competitive option in the mid-range smartphone market. Critics also appreciated the phone's clean software, which was free of the bloatware that often clutters devices from other manufacturers. The near-stock Android experience provided a smooth, intuitive interface that was easy to navigate.

From a consumer perspective, the Nothing Phone (1) was equally well-received. The phone's distinct design and user-friendly features attracted a strong following, particularly among tech enthusiasts who were eager for something different in a market dominated by a few major players. Many consumers were drawn to the phone's minimalist approach and its focus on functionality over unnecessary features. The customizability of the Glyph Interface was another selling point, as it allowed users to personalize their experience and interact with their devices in a more intuitive way.

Despite its many strengths, the Nothing Phone (1) was not without its criticisms. Some reviewers noted that the camera, while good, did not match the performance of flagship phones like those from Apple or Samsung. Battery life, while decent, was also an area where the phone could have performed better. However, these critiques did not overshadow the overall positive reception, and many felt that the phone offered exceptional value for its price.

Overall, the Nothing Phone (1) was seen as a bold and successful first entry into the smartphone market. It captured the attention of both tech reviewers and

Carl Pei

consumers with its innovative design, smooth performance, and user-centered features. The phone's release helped solidify Nothing as a brand to watch in the coming years, with the potential to reshape the way we think about smartphones.

Chapter 7

The Anticipation – Nothing Phone (3)

The smartphone market is often characterized by small, incremental improvements, but every now and then, a new release shakes things up. This was precisely what the Nothing Phone (3) promised to do, capturing the attention of both the tech community and general consumers. Building on the success of Nothing's previous releases, particularly the Nothing Phone (1) and (2), the Nothing Phone (3) was expected to continue the company's tradition of redefining what smartphones could be. Carl Pei's vision for the company was clear: to offer a product that was both functionally innovative and aesthetically unique.

The excitement surrounding the Nothing Phone (3) was not just about another new smartphone hitting the market.

Carl Pei

It was a reflection of how the Nothing brand had grown into something much bigger than just a tech company. The brand's ability to capture attention, innovate beyond conventional designs, and create an emotional connection with its audience created a sense of anticipation. This was more than a phone—it was a statement, one that would challenge the status quo of the smartphone industry.

The road to the announcement of the Nothing Phone (3) was one that had been paved with deliberate decisions and strategic moves. After the release of the Nothing Phone (1) and (2), both of which received praise for their unique design and user-centered features, the anticipation for the Phone (3) grew steadily. From the very beginning, Carl Pei's vision for Nothing was to create products that went beyond the traditional smartphone experience. With every release, Nothing was steadily building a reputation for offering high-quality, innovative products that stood out for their design, simplicity, and focus on user experience.

Carl Pei

The success of the Nothing Ear (1) earbuds, which set a new standard for wireless audio products, helped Nothing carve out its niche in the tech industry. The company's philosophy of combining cutting-edge technology with a simple, minimalist design had garnered significant attention and loyalty from consumers who were looking for something different from the tech giants. By the time the Nothing Phone (3) was in development, there was already a solid foundation of consumers eager to see what the company would do next.

What made the journey leading to the Nothing Phone (3) so compelling was the consistent evolution of the brand. With each new product, the company built upon what came before, refining its design language, user experience, and innovation. For Pei and his team, it was not just about creating another smartphone; it was about continuing the brand's story and advancing their mission to deliver products that resonated deeply with users. Nothing was positioning itself as a brand that would continue to push boundaries and redefine what smartphones could be, and the Phone (3) was the next step in that mission.

The marketing campaign leading up to the phone's announcement was highly anticipated in itself. Nothing had already established a reputation for its direct, authentic approach to marketing, and as with previous product releases, the announcement of the Phone (3) was expected to generate a significant amount of buzz. The company strategically built hype, teasing new features and making subtle announcements that hinted at the direction the phone would take. These efforts helped fuel the growing sense of excitement, creating a palpable anticipation for the official launch.

As the announcement of the Nothing Phone (3) approached, the expectations surrounding the device were exceptionally high. Having already established a reputation for delivering products that combined cutting-edge technology with thoughtful design, Nothing had set the bar for its future releases. Consumers and tech enthusiasts alike were eager to see how the Nothing Phone (3) would continue this legacy and what new innovations it would bring to the table.

One of the primary expectations surrounding the Nothing Phone (3) was that it would maintain the brand's focus on design. The transparent back design, which had become iconic with the Phone (1), had been a standout feature, and many wondered how Nothing would evolve this concept. The Phone (3) was expected to either enhance this transparency or introduce new design elements that would continue the company's reputation for unique and visually striking aesthetics. The transparent back had already become synonymous with Nothing's approach to technology, and fans anticipated that the company would refine this feature even further, whether through enhanced materials, innovative tech integration, or new ways of displaying internal components.

Carl Pei

The Glyph Interface, which featured customizable LED lights on the back of the phone, was another expected feature to be further developed in the Nothing Phone (3). This interface had made a big impression on users of the previous models, offering a visually interactive way to receive notifications and alerts. There were high expectations that Nothing would expand upon this feature, perhaps offering more customization options or adding more functionality to this unique element. The expectation was that the Glyph Interface would become more integrated into the overall user experience, offering even greater ways for consumers to personalize their devices.

Performance was another area where there were elevated expectations. The Nothing Phone (1) and (2) had already offered impressive specs for their price range, and many consumers hoped that the Phone (3) would continue this trend. Expectations included a faster processor, a high-refresh-rate display, an improved camera system, and better battery life—all without compromising on design. The smartphone market is constantly evolving, and users were eager to see how the Nothing Phone (3) could keep up with its competitors in terms of hardware while maintaining the brand's signature design and usability. Many believed that the Phone (3) would need to offer flagship-level performance in certain areas to continue building Nothing's reputation as a premium yet affordable alternative to larger smartphone brands.

Battery life, fast charging, and other functional aspects were also anticipated to improve with the Phone (3). Users who had come to expect a high level of performance from Nothing's earlier models were eager to see if the Phone (3) could deliver even more in terms of longevity and charging speed. In an era when smartphones are used for nearly everything—from productivity tasks to entertainment and social media—battery life is a crucial factor for many users, and the Phone (3) would need to meet these demands.

In addition to hardware and design, another key expectation was the continued refinement of the user experience. Nothing had made a name for itself by offering a near-stock Android experience with minimal bloatware, and consumers hoped that the Phone (3) would continue to provide a clean, efficient software environment. The Phone (3) would need to balance customization with simplicity, offering users a seamless experience that allowed them to interact with their devices intuitively.

The Nothing Phone (3) had the potential to be more than just another smartphone. It was poised to continue the company's commitment to creating products that not only offered top-tier performance but also challenged the established norms of smartphone design and usage. The uniqueness of the Phone (3) lay in its ability to blend advanced technology with a design philosophy that emphasized simplicity and user-centered innovation.

Carl Pei

One of the key differentiators of the Nothing Phone (3) was its continued emphasis on design. The transparent back design, while already a signature of the brand, was likely to evolve further in the Phone (3). This transparent aesthetic had set Nothing apart from other brands in the market, and the expectation was that the company would push the boundaries even further. Whether through the use of new materials, more advanced technology embedded within the transparent elements, or further refinement of the internal components that were on display, the Nothing Phone (3) was expected to be a bold and visually striking device.

The Glyph Interface, another defining feature of Nothing phones, also had the potential to become even more interactive and personalized. The Phone (3) was expected to build on the existing functionality, allowing users to customize the LED light patterns more extensively. The innovation of combining form and function in this way was a unique selling point, and the Phone (3) was anticipated to continue this trend, adding even more practical uses for the Glyph Interface while enhancing its visual appeal.

Beyond design, the Nothing Phone (3) had the potential to disrupt the smartphone market by offering flagship-level performance at a more affordable price. In a market where high-end smartphones are often priced out of reach for many consumers, the Nothing Phone (3) could continue the brand's strategy of offering premium features without the premium price tag. Its combination of powerful specs, innovative design, and reasonable pricing could further establish Nothing as a viable alternative to the likes of Apple, Samsung, and Google, especially for those seeking a unique smartphone experience without the inflated costs.

Another way the Nothing Phone (3) had the potential to disrupt the market was through its software. The clean, near-stock Android experience that Nothing offered with its previous models was highly regarded, and many expected the Phone (3) to continue this trend while adding new features and improvements. The balance between customization and simplicity in the software interface could help Nothing stand out in an industry where software often feels bogged down by unnecessary features and bloatware. Consumers were likely to appreciate the streamlined, efficient experience that the Phone (3) was expected to provide.

The phone's user-centric approach, which focused on making technology intuitive and approachable, was another factor that set it apart. By continuing to emphasize simplicity, personalization, and thoughtful design, the Nothing Phone (3) had the potential to appeal to a wide range of consumers—tech enthusiasts, everyday users, and those who wanted something different from the conventional smartphones on the market.

Ultimately, the Nothing Phone (3) had the potential to challenge the way we think about smartphones. By blending design with functionality, performance with simplicity, and affordability with premium features, the

Carl Pei

Nothing Phone (3) could set a new standard in the industry. The phone's potential to disrupt the market lay not just in its hardware and software but in its ability to offer consumers a new, more human-centric approach to technology. The Phone (3) had all the ingredients to be a true game-changer in the smartphone space.

Chapter 8

A Glimpse into His Life – Carl Pei the Man

Carl Pei, known for his pioneering work with OnePlus and his current venture, Nothing, has become a figure synonymous with innovation in the tech world. While his professional achievements are well-known, there is much more to Carl Pei than his role as a tech entrepreneur. His personal life, the values that guide him, his passions, and the relationships he cherishes provide insight into the man behind the tech mogul. Pei's story is one of ambition and dedication, but also of the principles and experiences that have shaped him into the visionary leader he is today.

Though most people are familiar with Carl Pei's career, the human side of his journey is equally compelling. It is in the way he approaches life outside of work, his personal growth, and the relationships he maintains, where we see the true depth of his character. His values and passions have been integral not only to his personal life but also to how he builds and leads his companies. Understanding these aspects offers a more complete picture of Pei's evolution—not just as a businessman, but as a person.

Carl Pei's passion for technology and innovation is not only born from his professional ambitions but also from the values he was raised with and the experiences that shaped him outside of work. His journey to success, both in his personal life and career, has been guided by a strong sense of purpose and an appreciation for different perspectives. Having grown up in Stockholm, Sweden, with parents who had emigrated from China, Pei was exposed to a rich blend of cultural influences. This multicultural upbringing played a pivotal role in shaping his worldview, providing him with a diverse set of ideas and approaches that would later define how he saw the world and how he approached business.

Carl Pei

Pei's parents instilled in him the importance of discipline, focus, and resilience. The combination of his father's strong work ethic and his mother's creative influence gave him a balanced foundation of both pragmatism and creativity. This dual perspective has been a defining characteristic of Pei's leadership style, especially when it comes to designing products and creating businesses that balance innovative thinking with practical solutions. He learned early on that to achieve success, one must be persistent, but also willing to adapt and change when necessary.

Beyond his upbringing, Carl Pei is deeply passionate about design, art, and creativity. His love for these areas is evident in the products he creates. For Pei, technology is not merely about functionality—it is an opportunity to merge creativity with utility. This passion for design and aesthetics is one of the reasons Nothing's products stand out in a crowded tech market. From the transparent design of the Nothing Ear (1) to the clean, minimalist look of the Nothing Phone (1), Pei has always believed that technology should not just be a tool, but something that enriches people's lives, offering both beauty and function.

While Pei's career has been deeply intertwined with technology, he also finds inspiration in other creative fields. His interest in fashion, for example, influences his approach to product design, where aesthetics and functionality work hand in hand. The way he blends innovation with a sense of style in his products reflects a broader passion for making everyday objects beautiful and practical.

One of Pei's core values is authenticity. He has made it clear in interviews and public statements that he believes in being transparent—not just with consumers but also with himself and those he works with. This value of openness extends to the way he leads his companies, as he prioritizes clear, honest communication with his team and his customers. His belief in transparency is not limited to product design but extends to the culture he fosters within his companies. For Pei, success is not just about innovation; it's about building trust and fostering meaningful relationships both within the workplace and beyond it.

Behind Carl Pei's professional success lies a network of strong personal relationships that have been crucial in shaping the person he is today. While Pei's work in the tech world has garnered him widespread recognition, his family and friendships have remained a source of strength and support throughout his career. Despite the intense demands of being a high-profile entrepreneur, Pei has always placed a high value on the people who matter most in his life.

Family plays an integral role in Pei's life. Raised in a multicultural environment, Pei's relationship with his parents has had a lasting influence on his approach to both business and life. His family, particularly his parents, taught him the value of hard work, dedication, and an unwavering commitment to his goals. Pei often credits his parents with instilling in him a deep sense of responsibility and an appreciation for the importance of perseverance, especially when faced with obstacles.

Pei's family also serves as a reminder of the importance of balance. While he is deeply passionate about his work, he recognizes the significance of maintaining strong personal bonds. Despite the global reach of his business endeavors, Pei always makes time for his family, often mentioning that they provide him with perspective and grounding. For Pei, success is not only measured by professional accomplishments but also by the strength of the relationships he has with those closest to him.

In addition to his family, Carl Pei has forged close friendships throughout his career. These relationships have helped him navigate the pressures of entrepreneurship and offered him emotional support when needed. Pei values friendships where there is mutual respect, trust, and the ability to challenge each other. These friendships have allowed him to grow personally and professionally, offering him a network of individuals who share his vision, values, and passion for innovation.

What stands out about Pei's approach to relationships is his authenticity. In a world where professional networks are often transactional, Pei emphasizes the importance of genuine connections. Whether with his team members, investors, or close friends, Pei's relationships are rooted in mutual respect, honesty, and shared values. This transparency in his personal life mirrors the culture he has cultivated at Nothing, where openness and collaboration are central tenets.

Despite his success and high-profile career, Pei remains approachable and grounded. He is not the stereotypical tech mogul who isolates himself behind closed doors; instead, he engages with his team, listens to feedback, and encourages open dialogue. His leadership style is a reflection of his belief in the power of human connections, and he strives to create a company culture where every individual feels valued and empowered.

Carl Pei

Carl Pei's approach to work-life balance is a topic that often comes up when discussing his personal philosophy. Like many entrepreneurs, Pei's life is full of demanding responsibilities, long hours, and the constant pressure to innovate. However, Pei has always emphasized the importance of finding a balance that allows him to focus on both his professional and personal life.

For Pei, work-life balance is not just about time management but about making intentional choices. He believes in focusing on quality over quantity, both in his work and personal life. While he is deeply committed to his work, he ensures that he spends quality time with family and close friends, which he believes is essential for his overall well-being. In interviews, Pei has mentioned that taking time to recharge and step away from work allows him to approach challenges with a fresh perspective and renewed creativity. This balance is crucial not only for his own health but also for the growth of his companies. Pei encourages his team to adopt similar practices, emphasizing that mental and physical well-being are important to sustain long-term productivity and innovation.

In terms of leadership, Carl Pei is known for his collaborative and inclusive style. He believes that leadership is not about issuing commands but about guiding and inspiring others to reach their full potential. His approach is rooted in the idea that a leader should empower those around them, creating an environment where everyone feels they can contribute and grow. Pei has built a culture at Nothing where transparency and open communication are prioritized, and where each team member is encouraged to bring their ideas to the table. He is known for leading by example, demonstrating humility, curiosity, and a willingness to learn from others.

Pei also believes that leadership requires emotional intelligence. In an industry that is often fast-paced and competitive, he stresses the importance of understanding and empathizing with others. This ability to connect with people on a deeper level is something Pei considers vital to his success. It has allowed him to foster a loyal and motivated team and build strong relationships with his consumers and business partners. Leadership, for Pei, is not just about making decisions but about creating a vision that others can rally behind and contributing to the growth of those around him.

Personal growth is another cornerstone of Pei's philosophy. He believes that the journey of self-improvement is ongoing and that there is always room to evolve. Even after achieving significant success, Pei remains committed to learning, adapting, and challenging himself. His willingness to embrace new challenges, learn from his mistakes, and grow as both a leader and an individual has been key to his continued success. He believes that true personal growth comes from pushing oneself out of one's comfort zone, and this mindset is something that has been essential in shaping both his professional and personal life.

Carl Pei

Pei also understands that growth is not just about career achievements but about becoming a better person. His focus on humility, empathy, and emotional intelligence allows him to lead with integrity and compassion. As he continues to innovate and expand his companies, Pei remains grounded in his personal values, always striving to be better not just in his work but in his personal life as well.

Chapter 9

The Evolution of Technology – Pei's Impact on the Smartphone Industry

The smartphone industry has been shaped by many pioneers, but few have made such a significant impact as Carl Pei. With his leadership at OnePlus and later at Nothing, Pei has played a crucial role in transforming the way consumers view and interact with technology. His work has redefined the smartphone experience, emphasizing not just innovation but simplicity, design, and a deeper connection to users. Through his vision, Pei has demonstrated that smartphones are not merely tools for communication—they are integral to our daily lives, meant to be both functional and beautiful.

Pei's approach to smartphone development has consistently focused on creating devices that prioritize the user experience. Instead of following the conventional trends of the industry, which often focus on adding more features and complexity, Pei's companies have strived to deliver simplicity without sacrificing performance. This commitment to thoughtful, user-centered design has allowed Pei to reshape the smartphone industry in meaningful ways. With the success of OnePlus and his later venture, Nothing, Pei's influence extends far beyond the products he has created, affecting the future of tech trends and the way we engage with technology on a daily basis.

Carl Pei's approach to technology is rooted in the belief that smartphones should not just be functional but should enrich the lives of their users. From his early days with OnePlus to the creation of Nothing, Pei has been a driving force in making smartphones more than just tools for communication. He has worked tirelessly to introduce a new way of thinking about smartphones—one that prioritizes simplicity, design, and innovation.

Carl Pei

At OnePlus, Pei's vision was clear from the beginning: create high-performance smartphones that offer value without compromising on design. With the launch of the OnePlus One in 2014, Pei and his team set out to build a phone that could compete with the best in the market while being more affordable. The OnePlus One combined top-tier specs with a relatively lower price point, challenging the industry's norms. But what truly set the phone apart was its user experience. OnePlus emphasized a near-stock version of Android, offering a clean interface without the bloatware commonly found in devices from other manufacturers. This approach resonated with users who wanted a seamless, unencumbered experience, and it laid the foundation for the brand's success.

However, Pei's vision extended far beyond just offering a budget-friendly flagship device. He understood that the smartphone market was increasingly saturated with similar devices, so differentiation through design and usability was crucial. OnePlus's minimalist approach to product design quickly became one of the brand's defining features. The focus was not just on hardware specifications but on creating a device that felt intuitive, accessible, and comfortable in the user's hand. This focus on design, paired with performance, helped OnePlus carve out a unique space in a market dominated by giants like Apple and Samsung.

Pei's commitment to design continued as he shifted focus to his new venture, Nothing. With Nothing, Pei set out to bring a fresh perspective to the tech industry. The transparent design of the Nothing Ear (1), which offered a window into the inner workings of the earbuds, was a direct reflection of the brand's ethos: transparency, simplicity, and beauty. The Nothing Phone (1) continued this design philosophy with a transparent back that allowed users to see the phone's components, creating an immediate connection between the device and the user. This design innovation set the brand apart in a crowded market, where most phones look nearly identical.

Carl Pei

At the heart of Nothing's design is the belief that technology should not just perform well but should also be aesthetically pleasing and user-friendly. This approach has challenged the typical smartphone design conventions, where functionality often takes precedence over form. Pei's ability to merge form and function has led to a new type of smartphone, one that is designed to be beautiful and efficient, not just a tool but an experience. The Glyph Interface, a unique feature on the Nothing Phone (1), further exemplifies Pei's commitment to enhancing the user experience. By integrating customizable LED lights on the back of the phone, Pei introduced a new way to interact with smartphones that is both visually appealing and practical.

Through his vision, Carl Pei has consistently proven that smartphones can be both high-performing and beautiful. His emphasis on simplicity and design, alongside innovation, has shaped the way we view technology, offering a refreshing alternative to the overcomplicated, feature-heavy devices that had long dominated the market.

Carl Pei's influence on the smartphone industry goes beyond the products he has released. Through his work with OnePlus and Nothing, Pei has set in motion a series of broader tech trends that continue to shape the future of the industry. His commitment to simplicity, transparency, and design has made a lasting impact on how tech companies approach product development, marketing, and user engagement.

One of the most significant trends that Pei has helped influence is the emphasis on design in the technology space. As smartphones became increasingly ubiquitous, their designs often became secondary to their technical specifications. However, Pei's work at OnePlus and Nothing has demonstrated that design is just as important as performance. By focusing on creating devices that are aesthetically pleasing and easy to use, Pei has led the charge in bringing design back to the forefront of product development. This trend is now evident across the industry, with even major brands like Apple and Samsung investing heavily in the design of their devices, from materials to user interfaces.

The focus on transparency and user engagement is another trend that Pei has helped establish. With Nothing, Pei made a bold statement by introducing transparent devices that allowed users to see the inner components of their phones and earbuds. This design choice not only set Nothing apart but also communicated a message of openness and honesty. In a market where many companies hide the inner workings of their products, Nothing's transparency has inspired other companies to reconsider how they communicate with their consumers. As consumers become more conscious of the ethics behind their purchasing decisions, transparency in product design and business practices is likely to become an increasingly important trend in the tech industry.

Additionally, Pei's work has contributed to the growing trend of user-centric technology. Many companies in the tech world focus on adding more features and specifications, but Pei has emphasized that the best technology is the one that's most intuitive and accessible. By creating products that prioritize the user experience, Pei has helped shift the industry's focus away from features for the sake of features and toward products that genuinely enhance the lives of users. This shift is likely to continue, with more companies focusing on how their products make the user feel rather than simply how they perform.

Pei's impact on tech trends also extends to the growing demand for affordable yet high-quality smartphones. Through OnePlus, Pei proved that it was possible to offer flagship-level devices at a fraction of the price of other premium brands. This disrupted the market and forced other manufacturers to reconsider their pricing strategies. With Nothing, Pei has continued this trend by offering high-end design and performance at a competitive price point, making quality smartphones more accessible to a wider audience. As consumers increasingly demand more value for their money, the trend toward affordable yet premium devices will likely continue to influence the smartphone market.

Carl Pei's contributions to the smartphone industry, particularly through OnePlus and Nothing, have left an indelible mark on the market. Both companies have made significant contributions to the evolution of mobile technology, and their influence continues to be felt today. Through OnePlus, Pei introduced the idea that high-quality smartphones could be offered at a more affordable price, forcing other companies to rethink their pricing structures and value propositions. This shift in the market has had long-lasting effects, as more brands have followed in OnePlus's footsteps, offering devices that are both powerful and reasonably priced.

OnePlus also played a crucial role in fostering a new kind of consumer culture in the tech world. By emphasizing community engagement and customer loyalty, OnePlus set itself apart from other smartphone brands. Pei and his team understood the importance of building relationships with customers, not just selling them products. OnePlus's success was not just about creating a great phone—it was about creating a brand that resonated with people and made them feel like they were part of something bigger. This approach has since been adopted by other companies, further shaping the future of consumer-tech relationships.

The launch of Nothing marked a new chapter for Pei, but it also represented the next phase in his vision to change the smartphone industry. With Nothing, Pei continued to challenge the status quo by offering products that emphasized design, simplicity, and transparency. The Nothing Phone (1) and the Nothing Ear (1) have set new benchmarks for innovation in the industry, particularly with the introduction of features like the Glyph Interface. Nothing's commitment to creating products that are both aesthetically pleasing and user-friendly has resonated with consumers, and the company's influence on the industry is already being felt.

Pei's legacy in the smartphone industry will likely be defined by his ability to challenge conventions and create products that resonate with users on a deeper level. His focus on design, simplicity, and transparency has set a new standard for the industry, encouraging other companies to reconsider how they approach product development. Both OnePlus and Nothing have shown that technology can be both beautiful and functional, offering a more holistic and engaging experience for users.

Looking to the future, Pei's contributions will continue to influence the direction of the smartphone industry. The trends he has set in motion—such as prioritizing user experience, offering high-quality devices at an affordable price, and focusing on design—are likely to define the next generation of smartphones. As technology continues to evolve, Pei's vision for a more human-centered,

Carl Pei

transparent, and aesthetically thoughtful tech world will
remain a driving force.

Chapter 10

Looking Ahead – The Future Beyond Nothing

In a world where technology advances at a rapid pace, few companies have managed to capture the imagination of consumers quite like Nothing. Founded by Carl Pei, the company has quickly established a reputation for creating products that challenge industry norms. From the iconic transparent design of the Nothing Ear (1) to the groundbreaking Glyph Interface in the Nothing Phone (1), the brand has redefined what smartphones and tech products can be, blending simplicity, design, and functionality.

Despite the early success, the journey for Nothing is just beginning. With the rapidly evolving tech landscape, the company finds itself at a crucial crossroads. While

Nothing has carved a distinct identity, the future holds endless possibilities for expansion, innovation, and disruption. As we look ahead, it is clear that the potential for Nothing's growth is vast—not just in terms of the products it will release but also in the larger impact it will have on the technology market as a whole.

Looking toward the future, the possibilities for Nothing seem boundless. The company has already shaken up the tech industry with its commitment to innovation and distinctive design, but there is still much to explore. As Nothing continues to grow, it's clear that the future will include new technologies, products, and potential markets that can help the company expand its reach and influence even further.

One of the most exciting areas for Nothing to explore is the audio market. The Nothing Ear (1) earbuds were a significant success, offering both unique design and strong performance at an affordable price. Given the popularity of the Ear (1) and the ongoing consumer interest in wireless audio products, it's not difficult to imagine Nothing expanding its presence in this space. The company could introduce new iterations of the Ear (1), or even diversify into entirely new audio categories, such as premium over-ear headphones or more advanced audio solutions for home use. As more consumers embrace wireless and integrated audio products, the opportunity for Nothing to establish itself as a key player in the audio market is clear.

In addition to audio products, the smart home industry is another area where Nothing could expand. As technology becomes increasingly integrated into the home, there is growing demand for smart devices that offer both high functionality and sleek design. With Pei's proven ability to blend aesthetics with practicality, Nothing is well-positioned to create smart home products that set new standards. Whether it's smart lighting, voice-controlled home assistants, or connected devices that seamlessly integrate with other tech products, the smart home market offers significant room for innovation. As more consumers seek cohesive and intuitive ecosystems, Nothing could leverage its design-focused philosophy to create products that are as beautiful as they are functional, leading to greater integration of its technology into daily life.

Wearable tech is another potential area of growth for Nothing. With the increasing popularity of fitness trackers, smartwatches, and health-focused devices, the wearable market offers substantial opportunities. Nothing could branch into creating devices that track health metrics, assist with fitness goals, or offer additional features like biometric monitoring. In an age where personal wellness and convenience are becoming top priorities, Nothing could differentiate itself by offering products that look just as good as they function. For instance, a smartwatch from Nothing could carry the same clean design language and emphasis on user experience as their other products, making it not only a tech tool but also a stylish accessory.

The smartphone market itself is also evolving. As consumers demand more from their devices, future iterations of the Nothing Phone could integrate cutting-edge technologies like augmented reality (AR), virtual reality (VR), and advanced artificial intelligence (AI) to offer new ways for users to interact with their environments. There is significant potential for Nothing to lead in this space, integrating AR and AI into the phone experience. By offering more immersive capabilities, Nothing could reshape how we use our smartphones, making them even more essential to our daily lives.

Another possible direction for the company involves developing its own operating system (OS). While Nothing currently uses Android as its base, creating a custom OS would allow the company to control the user experience even more directly. With a tailored OS, Nothing could deliver enhanced features, improved integration with other products, and a smoother, more intuitive experience for users. This could further differentiate the brand and ensure that Nothing products work in harmony, creating a cohesive ecosystem for consumers.

In addition to these product categories, the development of artificial intelligence (AI)-driven technologies could allow Nothing to offer devices that adapt to users' habits, making them smarter and more personalized. As AI continues to shape the future of technology, Nothing's focus on user-centered design could play a pivotal role in how AI is integrated into consumer products. By developing products that learn from users and improve over time, Nothing could make technology feel more intuitive and less like a tool, and more like a partner in users' everyday lives.

With each of these potential areas of growth, Nothing's future looks filled with opportunities for innovation. Whether expanding into new product categories or embracing next-generation technologies, the company has positioned itself to be a significant player in the evolving tech landscape. The possibilities are vast, and with Carl

Carl Pei

Pei at the helm, the company is set to continue challenging industry conventions and driving the future of consumer technology.

Carl Pei's leadership will continue to be a defining factor in the future of Nothing, as well as in the broader tech industry. Pei has proven himself to be a visionary leader, one who is not afraid to take risks and disrupt established norms. From his work with OnePlus to his creation of Nothing, Pei has consistently shown an ability to identify gaps in the market and seize opportunities for innovation.

Pei's approach to leadership is marked by a unique blend of humility, transparency, and boldness. His success at OnePlus, where he helped build a brand that became synonymous with value and performance, was based on his ability to think beyond the product itself and focus on creating a relationship with consumers. This philosophy carried over into Nothing, where Pei has fostered a brand that prioritizes transparency, user feedback, and community-building. As the company continues to grow, Pei's leadership style will undoubtedly play a central role in shaping the company's culture, direction, and future products.

At Nothing, Pei's ongoing role is not just about overseeing product development—he is also a driving force behind the company's vision for the future. His deep understanding of consumer behavior, technology trends, and market dynamics makes him an invaluable figure in the industry. As the company expands into new product categories and technologies, Pei's leadership will be critical in guiding the company through new challenges and opportunities. His ability to inspire his team and keep them focused on the core values of simplicity, design, and innovation will help Nothing maintain its identity as it grows.

Pei's influence extends far beyond the confines of his company. As a prominent figure in the tech world, he will continue to inspire other entrepreneurs and industry leaders. His work at OnePlus revolutionized the smartphone market, and his continued innovation at Nothing is poised to do the same for the next generation of tech products. Pei's ideas about the future of technology—particularly his focus on user experience, simplicity, and design—will continue to shape the broader conversation about how tech products are developed, marketed, and used.

As the tech world looks to the future, Carl Pei will remain a significant figure in shaping the direction of the industry. His leadership, creativity, and commitment to innovation will ensure that he remains at the forefront of the industry for years to come.

As we look to the future, it's fascinating to speculate where Carl Pei and Nothing might go next in the ever-evolving tech landscape. Pei has already established himself as a disruptive force in the industry, and the journey of Nothing has only just begun. So, where will he take the company in the coming years?

Carl Pei

One possibility is the continued expansion into new product categories. While Nothing's first products—the Nothing Ear (1) and Nothing Phone (1)—have already made an impact, there is still significant room for growth. As mentioned earlier, wearables, smart home technology, and even health-focused devices could be potential areas for Nothing to explore. With a focus on simplicity and seamless integration, Nothing has the potential to create a new ecosystem of devices that work together effortlessly, making users' lives easier and more enjoyable.

Another area where Nothing could make a big impact is in augmented reality (AR). As AR technology becomes more advanced, there is increasing interest in how it can be integrated into everyday consumer products. Given Nothing's commitment to creating innovative and engaging user experiences, it would not be surprising to see the company explore AR in its future smartphones, wearables, or even new devices. AR could open up new possibilities for how users interact with their digital and physical worlds, and Pei's vision for the future of tech could play a key role in making this a reality.

Carl Pei may also continue to challenge the traditional approaches to business and consumer engagement. His work with OnePlus and Nothing has been marked by a focus on building a strong connection with consumers, and as the tech world shifts towards more personalized and transparent brands, Pei's approach may continue to set the tone for how companies build relationships with their customers. With more emphasis on transparency, sustainability, and ethical business practices, Pei could lead the charge in making these values a core part of the tech industry's future.

As for Pei's personal role in the tech industry, it's likely that he will continue to serve as a thought leader, sharing his insights on innovation, product design, and the future of consumer tech. His experience as a founder and his ability to create products that resonate with users will position him as a go-to figure for discussions on the future of technology. Whether through speaking engagements, mentorship, or involvement in new projects, Pei's influence will extend beyond the walls of Nothing.

Conclusion

As we reach the conclusion of this book, I want to take a moment to thank you for choosing to read it. Whether you've picked it up to gain insights into Carl Pei's revolutionary approach to technology, to learn from his work with Nothing, or simply to explore the ideas within these pages, your time and engagement are deeply appreciated. Writing this book wasn't merely about presenting facts—it was about offering you a perspective that encourages deeper thinking and an understanding of the impact technology has on our world. I hope that by the time you've finished reading, you'll walk away with a sense of clarity and inspiration.

In this book, we've followed Carl Pei's journey—one that has been marked by a relentless pursuit of innovation. From co-founding OnePlus and disrupting the smartphone industry to launching Nothing and shaking up consumer tech, Pei's work has continually challenged the status quo. His story isn't just about creating groundbreaking products; it's about rethinking what technology means and how it should function in our everyday lives. Through each chapter, we've witnessed how vision, resilience, and bold decision-making can lead to products that don't just satisfy a market need but change the way we interact with technology.

The lessons we've drawn from Pei's career are applicable far beyond the tech industry. They remind us that true progress comes not from merely following existing paths but from questioning them. Technology today is evolving faster than ever, and those who want to stay relevant must be willing to challenge assumptions and embrace new ways of thinking. Pei's leadership has shown us that simplicity and user-centric design are as powerful as any technological advancement. In an age when devices are becoming more complex, his approach reminds us that the simplest solutions often make the most meaningful impact.

Carl Pei

As the world of technology continues to shift, it's easy to get caught up in the race for the latest gadget or feature. But Pei's philosophy teaches us that real innovation doesn't just come from new features—it comes from understanding people's needs and creating products that enhance their daily experiences. Whether it's smartphones, wearables, or audio technology, the key to success is not about overwhelming users with options, but rather creating something that truly speaks to their desires and simplifies their interactions with the digital world.

Looking forward, the potential for Nothing is limitless. With the foundation that's been laid in these early years, the company has the opportunity to grow and evolve in ways that will shape the future of consumer technology. New product categories such as wearables, smart home devices, and even AI-driven tech are just the beginning. As technology becomes more integrated into our lives, brands that can create seamless, functional, and beautiful ecosystems will lead the charge. Nothing is already on the path to defining what's next in consumer electronics, and

I'm excited to see how they continue to push boundaries and create innovative solutions that resonate with a global audience.

Carl Pei, too, remains a key figure in the tech world. His influence is far-reaching, and it's clear that his ability to lead with authenticity, vision, and humility will continue to inspire. His work has not only redefined what a smartphone can be but has also set new standards for leadership in tech companies. As Nothing continues to grow and expand into new product categories, Pei's approach to leadership will undoubtedly continue to influence how other companies approach innovation and consumer engagement.

What's perhaps most exciting about Pei's work is his ability to adapt to the constantly changing landscape of technology. He's demonstrated a keen sense of the trends that will define the next generation of products, from design aesthetics to user interaction. And as he continues to lead Nothing forward, I'm sure we'll see even more innovations that shape the way we interact with the technology around us.

But beyond his work with Nothing, Pei's story serves as an inspiration for anyone looking to make an impact in their own field. Whether you're an entrepreneur, a tech enthusiast, or simply someone interested in understanding the broader forces shaping our world, the lessons learned from Pei's career are universal. The ability to think critically, challenge existing paradigms, and maintain a deep focus on user experience are skills that transcend industries. As technology continues to evolve, these principles will remain at the core of successful innovation.

As you reflect on the ideas presented in this book, I encourage you to consider how you might apply them to your own endeavors. Whether you are looking to innovate in technology, business, or any other field, Carl Pei's journey offers a roadmap for those who want to make a meaningful difference. The world is changing at a rapid pace, and there are endless opportunities for anyone with a clear vision, a willingness to take risks, and the determination to push forward.

Your feedback means the world to me, and I'd love to hear your thoughts on this book. If you found the information here useful, thought-provoking, or inspiring, I would greatly appreciate it if you could share your experience with an honest review on Amazon. Your review not only helps others find this book but also provides valuable insights that will make future editions even better. Your feedback, whether it's about how the book resonated with you or suggestions for improvement, will be instrumental in shaping the next steps for this work. I am committed to delivering content that resonates and provides value, and your input is vital in making that happen.

If you have any thoughts on areas where this book could improve or any suggestions for new topics to explore, I am all ears. Your honest reviews and feedback will make future editions more insightful and comprehensive. Your voice matters, and it plays an important role in making sure this book continues to meet the needs of readers like you.

As technology evolves, so too does the need for understanding how we, as individuals, engage with the tools that shape our lives. Pei's work serves as a reminder that technology isn't just about innovation for innovation's sake—it's about creating products that improve the human experience. The principles of simplicity, transparency, and user-centered design are not just trends; they are the building blocks of the future. As we look ahead, the opportunities for further innovation are limitless, and it's clear that Pei's influence will continue to shape the future of technology for many years to come.

Thank you again for reading this book. Your decision to engage with the content means more than you know, and I trust that you'll take away valuable insights as you move forward in your own journey. Technology is an ever-evolving field, and with visionaries like Carl Pei at the helm of the next generation of tech companies, the future is bright. I hope this book has provided you not only with a deeper understanding of the role of innovation in technology but also with a fresh perspective on the impact of design, leadership, and human-centered thinking in shaping the products that will define our world.

The journey does not end here—if anything, it's just beginning. As we continue to navigate the fast-paced world of technology, remember that we all have the ability to shape the future. Whether you're an innovator, a creator, or a consumer, your choices and actions will contribute to the next wave of technological advancements. The future is full of possibility, and I hope you leave this book with a sense of excitement and purpose for what lies ahead.

Thank you for being part of this journey. I look forward to hearing your thoughts, and I'm excited to see where your own path in technology will take you.

Carl Pei

www.ingramcontent.com/pod-product-compliance
Lightning Source LLC
LaVergne TN
LVHW051659050326
832903LV00032B/3895